European Council of Internationa
Council of International Sch

Effective International Schools Series

Governance
in International Schools

edited by

Adèle Hodgson

Matthew Chuck

Peridot Press

First published in 2005 by Peridot Press,
a division of John Catt Educational Ltd
Great Glemham, Saxmundham, Suffolk IP17 2DH
Tel: +44 (0) 1728 663668 Fax: +44 (0) 1728 663415
E–mail: info@peridot.co.uk Internet: http://www.peridot.co.uk

Opinions expressed in this publication are those of the contributors, and are not necessarily those of the
publishers or the sponsors. We cannot accept responsibility for any errors or omissions.

The Sex Discrimination Act 1975. The publishers have taken all reasonable steps to avoid a
contravention of Section 38 of the Sex Discrimination Act 1975. However, it should be noted that (save
where there is an express provision to the contrary) where words have been used which denote the
masculine gender only, they shall, pursuant and subject to the said Act, for the purpose of this
publication, be deemed to include the feminine gender and vice versa.

A CIP catalogue record for this book is available from the British Library.

ISBN:1 904724 29 9

Designed and typeset by Peridot Press, a division of John Catt Educational Limited,
Great Glemham, Saxmundham, Suffolk IP17 2DH

Printed and bound in Great Britain by Bell and Bain Ltd, Glasgow, Scotland

Table of Contents

Foreword   Effective International Schools Series 4

About the Authors   5

Preface   6

Chapter One: Introduction to the world of governance 7
                      Adèle Hodgson

Chapter Two: The board and best practice 12
                      Richard Tangye

Chapter Three: The board and strategic planning 17
                      Matthew Chuck

Chapter Four: The board and operations 21
                      Matthew Chuck

Chapter Five: The board and its committees 25
                      Matthew Chuck

Chapter Six: The board and the head of school 30
                      Don Vinge

Chapter Seven: The board and managing conflict 37
                      Wilf Stout

Chapter Eight: The board and evaluation 44
                      Adèle Hodgson

Chapter Nine: Final review 48
                      Adèle Hodgson

Appendix   Useful evaluation tools 50

Foreword:
Effective International
Schools Series

ECIS/CIS are not-for-profit organisations dedicated to the advancement of internationalism through education by the provision of services to their members.

ECIS/CIS member schools are spread around the globe and are immensely varied in nature. Yet any of them, new or established, large or small, day or boarding, co-educational or single sex, monocultural or multicultural, can aspire to developing internationally-minded students. The sole proviso, as expressed in the ECIS Statement of Philosophy, is that they are committed to the promotion of an international outlook amongst all members of their communities.

ECIS and CIS see their roles as providing services, which actively assist schools in working towards this ideal, through practical support. The Effective International schools series is one way of doing this.

For the purposes of this series, ECIS/CIS will restrict themselves to those areas of a school's operation with regard to which the Councils are in a position to offer sound practical support in the form of documents which offer reliable guidelines and proven examples of good practice. There is much to be gained from sharing the experiences of member schools and little to be gained from reinventing the wheel. Much has been learned since ECIS was founded and time, energy and money are too precious to waste. The experience of other schools may offer a real head start.

Each publication will, therefore, have the following elements in common:

- They are driven by a common set of beliefs and values about student learning with an international outlook;
- They are structured so as to illustrate a logical progression from profile to policy to practice;
- They are based on successful experience in International schools, but offer suggestions generic enough to apply in a variety of contexts.

ECIS and CIS trust this series will prove useful to members and welcome any suggestions for improvements to each publication or for additions to the series.

Kevin Bartlett is Director of
the International School of Brussels, Belgium.

About the Authors

Adèle Hodgson was born in the United Kingdom and studied at the Universities of London and Strathclyde. Most of Adèle's career has been spent working abroad in the fields of strategic planning, marketing and public relations. Her experience spans the business and not-for-profit worlds ranging from banking to medical research to education. She works at Frankfurt International School and is a regular advisor to other International schools on marketing, governance and strategic planning. She is a co-author of two books on strategic planning and a frequent speaker at international education conferences, and a member of the ECIS Committees on Governance and Development.

Matthew Chuck is also British, and a science graduate from Cambridge University. Before setting up his own consultancy, he was a senior commercial manager with one of America's most successful materials companies, based in Frankfurt. Matthew developed his interest in international education both as a parent and as a trustee of Frankfurt International School, in which role he participated in several long-term projects in various capacities, including treasurer. Matthew is the co-author of *Strategic Planning in International Schools*.

Wilf Stout has completed thirty-five years in education in UK independent and state schools; on the staff of the University of Cambridge; and as the founding director of two International schools: the International School of South Africa and the International School of Cape Town. He is the author of numerous textbooks and is a regular lecturer and speaker on educational topics. Wilf is a team member for CIS Accreditation Teams and the Strategic Planning Work Group for the Alliance of International Education. He is currently completing his doctorate at the University of Bath and is Director of Curriculum for GEMS.

Richard Tangye is the Executive Director of CIS. Richard has a degree in economics and politics from Cambridge University and, after a brief spell teaching in Papua New Guinea, joined the world of business. After working in North America for ten years, he has spent the past sixteen years with Jardine Matheson in Asia where, in addition to his business responsibilities, he has actively participated in school governance, new school building and advisory bodies on education. He has been board chair at the British International School in Jakarta, Taipei European School in Taiwan, and the South Island School in Hong Kong. In this latter location he was a member of the Management Committee of the English School's Foundation, and chair of the Teacher's Pay Review Committee.

Don Vinge has enjoyed success in Europe as a principal, head of school, director and superintendent. In Canada he also served as principal and associate superintendent for the Edmonton Public Schools, a very large urban district recognised for its progressive and innovative approaches to governance, curriculum, and school-based decision-making and budgeting. He has worked with both elected and appointed school boards, and those with a mix of both. While in Europe, Don also served five years as a member and chair of the AFCENT International School Board. Presently, Don remains as a consultant for school development, organisation, programme audits and governance. His experience is particularly in demand for the establishment of new schools.

Preface

This book was the brainchild of Mike Maybury, former CEO of CIS, who wisely foresaw that governance in International schools was central to the development of these institutions. The purpose of the book is to provide a highly readable publication that will strengthen people's understanding of the role and responsibilities of trustees and their relationships with the other stakeholders in the school.

The total experience of the authors in the field of education is awe-inspiring. This experience has been gained on many different continents and in many different types of schools. The concept for the book was discussed and developed at different ECIS conferences – those precious occasions when educators from all over the world get together to challenge and discuss each others thoughts and ideas.

We acknowledge the people who have given us support and advice on this project, in particular Carol Morrow, Elementary School Principal at Frankfurt International School. We are also indebted to the authors in this field whose work we have consulted and acknowledged.

We hope that as a result of this book readers will have a clearer understanding of governance in International schools.

The Authors
August 2005

Chapter One

Introduction to the world of governance

School governance is a complex and sometimes emotional topic and in this book we plan to provide a straightforward and useful guide for board members, administrators and faculty.

To many of us the topic of governance in International schools has long been a subject of fierce debate as the various stakeholder groups in International schools struggle to find the ideal formula. Governance in schools has grown from trial and error and to quote John Carver "borrows from – but does not mimic management". The number of books written on International school governance is few and hopefully this book will fill a demonstrable gap in the support available to boards.

Sadly, schools frequently lurch from boards that micro manage, to those that purely rubber stamp senior administration recommendations. Proponents of change, frustrated by the sensitivity of the balance of power, frequently recommend new approaches, or variations on the current model. They argue that the world is rapidly changing and the challenges facing International schools, the size of their budgets and their responsibilities as an employer, have outgrown the most frequently used governance model taken from 19th and 20th Century philanthropy. When one reflects on the evolution of school administration in the last 100 years, the lack of a similar change in the approach to governance is remarkable. Most board members have too little time to become effective in their role and usually move on before they really understand the complexities of educational institutions. This lack of continuity means that there is little sense of history, planning is often cautious and short term in its vision.

Before discussing any further the topic of governance we need to ask the questions: what makes board trustees good trustees and what are the characteristics of effective governance? Hopefully the answers will help boards and administration to measure the gap between 'what they are now' and 'what they aspire to be'. We do not advocate in this book one point of view or another but try to present strategies for board trustees and administrators to consider. The following observations will hopefully act as useful guidelines:

- School governance is best executed by knowing and asking questions rather than by exercising authority.

- It demands a skilled and knowledgeable group of people.

- Trustees need to understand their purpose and demonstrate this in all they do.

- Trustees should understand and act to ensure that the school's objectives and strategies are met.

- Trustees should be truly accountable to those they represent and believe in transparency.

- Trustees should govern in the sense of establishing the school's goals; setting its policy and planning its strategy together with the school's stakeholders rather than trying to manage the school.

- Trustees should hold effective, regular and timely meetings.

- Meetings should always be minuted.

- Trustees should regularly evaluate their own performance against their set goals and invite the opinions of senior administrators.

- Trustees should annually evaluate the board chair's performance.

- Trustees should believe and demonstrate that a system of continuous improvement is integral to their role.

- Trustees should act in an integrated partnership with the head and the senior management team.

Governing boards have existed in schools in one form or another for centuries. Despite the fact that most International schools were started by private or corporate initiatives there has been a surprising failure in the start up phase to look beyond a basic approach to governance. This statement is not designed to undervalue the efforts of founding and existing boards of trustees, but rather to stress the fact that truly efficient and effective boards are rare. John Carver in his governance model quotes that 'boards tend to be, in fact, incompetent groups of competent people'. Many of the International schools in Europe were started in the 1950s and 1960s, and their founding fathers often neither perceived how they would grow, nor reflected too much about how they should be governed. Usually, the founders were the first board members, and their parent-dominated model, despite the inherent frequent turnover, is still the most common model.

Bearing this background in mind, the central purpose of this book is to provide the reader with substantial food for thought and to perhaps help schools and their boards through the labyrinth of twists and turns leading to board best practice. The book is unique in that the contributors are drawn from both senior school administrators, and past board members. This means that each writer when writing about the different aspects of governance will bring their own perspective and viewpoint based upon years of practical experience. The book will be controversial at times, but will always have at its core what we collectively feel is best practice. Our goal is to look at every aspect of a board's role and responsibilities, including board evaluation and board interaction with the school's stakeholders. Each chapter will deal with a different topic and will be pragmatic and concise in its recommendations. We then move on to offer some useful documentation that we hope will help to improve board work and board relationships.

A school's history, characteristics, location, legal restraints and ownership will affect the choice of governance model in use. No matter what this model is, the important factor must be a clear definition of the board's role that is understood by the board and all the school's stakeholders. In simplistic terms the board is where the ultimate school authority lies, but the operational interpretation of the school's mission and goals are delegated to the head of school. The head of school is the board's only appointee and he acts as the board's gateway to the school. There is a belief that the board/head of school relationship will automatically evolve and grow and that its roots lie in mutual trust and communication. Sadly, these are not always a given in a constantly changing environment. It is only through establishing a culture of collaboration that a partnership actually develops.

An important point to remember is that a board must act as one body, unless otherwise agreed. It is the board acting as one which is the voice of the school. Statements from individual board members without the support of the full board are not valid. Ideally the board should delegate to its committees the role of working with the head and senior administrators on specific issues such as finance, facilities and policy.

When first recruited few board members realise the important balance demanded between being legally responsible for the school and yet not being part of its day-to-day management. Rarely do board members have the opportunity to learn about the job before they start, and usually they leave before the school really benefits from their experience. In the corporate world individuals receive specific management training and learn on the job to prepare them for leadership. In the case of International schools preparation is often little more than perfunctory. Some schools do not invest in effective board training and evaluation, and often leave members to sink or swim. Frequently, board members learn the mantra that their role is not to become involved in operational issues, but sometimes the temptation to meddle in what seems to be the really interesting side of the school activities is too high. In some schools, it is the head of school who is in the driving seat and appears to control the board's involvement. This type of scenario is equally dysfunctional. Boards not only require training in the mechanics of the school and its programs but also in group relationships and decision-making in governance. Part of a trustee's commitment to leading a school should be the never ending dedication to learning what they need to know to be effective.

The board when it delegates to the head of school holds him or her responsible for the school's overall performance. In a subsequent chapter we will discuss the all-important relationship between the head and the board. Meanwhile let it suffice to say that the board is accountable for what the head of school does and must through clear goal setting, indicators, regular reports and benchmarking ensure that the job is well done.

Currently there are various forms of International schools:

- Proprietor/for profit schools.

- Not for profit schools.

- Business partnership schools.

Proprietor/for profit schools often have boards that are made up of the shareholders, or the shareholders plus appointed members. Such boards could possibly make decisions which are more dominated by the profit motive than the needs of their students. In some instances it is felt that this model does not offer enough checks and balances to safeguard against poor judgment and self-interests. Sometimes stakeholder involvement is discouraged and is more likely to be restricted to parent and social activities. In common with all types of International schools, proprietor schools do delegate to others the running of the school – namely the head. The Inter Community Schools in London and the British International School in Prague are excellent examples of this model. The owner of the Inter Community group of schools delegates to the superintendent the overall supervisory role and he in turn appoints the three heads with whom he works to manage the individual schools. This reliance on others to run the school requires the proprietor to give careful consideration to the principles of effective delegation and to ensure that the environment is conducive to successful management. In addition to this he has to ensure that his investment is protected. In the case of a group of investors owning a school it is important that the board policy manual reflects the original contract between the owners in relation to further investments and the sale of or transfer of shares.

Many of the new schools in Asia and the Middle East are proprietor or business partnership schools and it is essential that the process for governing these schools is articulated from day one. As investors are recruited, their role and responsibilities have to be clearly established in the principal agreement to found the school. One of the most important safeguards to effective governance in proprietor schools is the role of the accrediting bodies, who examine in depth the benefits and authenticity of the governance model in use.

The most common type of International school in Europe, however, is the not for profit model. This model theoretically ensures that the association owns the school but places the central power into the hands of a few chosen or elected individuals. The selection and success of these board members is a very inexact science and continues to be the number one reason for the resignation of heads of school and the ensuing aftereffects. Frequently the election of board members is the result of a popularity/visi-

bility vote rather than an acknowledgement of the individual's ability and experience. In some of these schools we also see the growth of appointed boards, or boards which are a mixture of elected and appointed members. Appointed board members do allow for greater continuity and facilitate the selection and appointment of the best.

Business partnership schools stem from the needs of a major employer/employers to recruit employees and their families from abroad. Sometimes these schools are located in remote and far-flung areas. Schools of this nature are either owned or established by companies such as Mercedes Benz and Siemens. In the case of Mercedes Benz a special educational trust has been established to govern these activities. Such schools normally have a self-perpetuating board recruited from the company and their nominees. The relationship between the administration and the owners is usually that of a partnership and there appears to be more continuity and fewer problems.

Key issues to remember

- It is important that boards identify and build on what they are doing well, and that within the school's strategic plan clear governance goals and sub-strategies exist.

- Boards must recognise the need to communicate and collaborate within the board and with the school's stakeholders.

- No board member should behave as if he or she was coroneted, and all board members should remember that they are part of two teams: the board itself, and the partnership with the school's senior administrators.

- At all times boards should think strategically and not operationally.

- Of key importance must be ongoing training throughout the year and a sense of accountability for actions taken.

- Senior administrators must learn to build on the strengths of their relationship with the board and to work effectively in an open manner with their board partners.

In addition to these points it is important for board members to remember that where fundraising plans are initiated board members are expected to make and solicit gifts. The important rule in effective fundraising is that you cannot solicit a donation if you have not given yourself. Being a board member is about leadership and increasingly companies, individuals and foundations will only give to schools where there is evidence of 100% board involvement.

Bibliography

John Carver Guide Series on Effective Board Governance. Jossey Banks.

Chapter Two

The board and best practice:
well-meaning amateurs or a *tour-de-force*?

In my first board appointment, there is absolutely no doubt that I was an amateur, and I was certainly well-meaning, although whether I ever became gifted is open to question. If any board member considers themselves a *tour-de-force*, the red flags should be waving, as an effective board requires that it is the board that is the *tour-de-force*, and not any one personality within it. Boards, particularly those in International schools with transient communities, can find it hard to achieve the cohesion necessary for true effectiveness, but a lot of the pain can be removed, and effectiveness achieved, through a structured, disciplined approach to the task.

It's easy to lose sight of what should be the true objective of all involved in the wider school community in which the board provides leadership. The objective must be to improve the learning environment for the students: all talk of 'process', 'partnership', 'efficiency', 'accountability' and the continuous stream of management – speak counts for nothing unless the outcome is manifested in an improvement in the willingness and ability of students to learn. This must be the sole determinant of an effective board, with strategic plans, budgets, and committees but a means to an end.

People are generally motivated to join school boards because they want to make a difference; occasionally that difference either relates to a personal agenda rather than the good of the community, or they join because of the perceived prestige that it brings. Minimising this risk brings us to the critical question of the constitution and selection of the board, an issue more often than not established in the Articles of Association of the school, whether it be a foundation or proprietary, and hence difficult to change. Where the ability exists, the board should exercise suitable due diligence in the selection of new members.

The board is a team, and teams – even poor teams – are recognised as being more effective than any single individual in managing complex issues. The team must strike a balance between its elements – the thinker, the consolidator, the finisher, the one-on-the-fringe – while representing the interests of the whole school community. It must also, critically, strike a balance between stability in policy, while being seen to be responsive and accountable to the community it serves. From this you may correctly imply that I am in favour neither of wholly appointed boards nor of wholly elected boards. The former runs the risk of being divorced from the community and being perceived as a self-perpetuated oligarchy, while the latter runs the risk of abrupt changes in policy to the inevitable detriment of the school and the prevalence of personal agendas.

The respondents to the board survey carried out by The Council of International schools (CIS) in 2004 showed:

- 23% were self-perpetuating;
- 23% fully elected;
- 13% fully appointed;
- 41% a combination of elected and appointed.

There is, however, a material difference between the average tenure of a member on a self-perpetuating board at 7.5 years with that of a member of a combination board at 2.8 years.

A school would not employ a teacher who had not been trained, but how many times have we seen board members taken on board with little or no training or exposure to the issues? Board training is an integral part of the accreditation requirements, but there remains a belief that because a person is interested in the school, he or she is familiar and comfortable with the norms of board practice, the parameters under which the board operates and the ongoing issues facing the school. I cannot emphasise sufficiently the importance of an effective training and orientation programme for new board members, as this is a – no, the – major factor in determining the effectiveness of the board.

The fundamentals of an effective board are clear, and have been promulgated with remarkable commonality by organisations as diverse as the National Association of Independent Schools and the National Staff Development Council, while following closely those more directly related to public companies. In summary, an effective board is one which the members:

- Work together by consensus, while not being afraid to debate contentious issues.
- Leave any personal agendas outside the boardroom door.
- Are responsive to the views of others, and leave any disagreement within the confines of the meeting.
- Leave the management of the school to those entrusted with its task.
- Retain strict confidentiality of all discussions.
- Maintain a sense of proportion and a sense of humour.
- Set objectives for the board and evaluate themselves against those objectives.
- Retain clear focus on their objective to improve the learning environment for students.

At the risk of stating the obvious: to be effective the board has to meet. The CIS Annual Board Governance Survey reflects boards that meet three times each year, to those that hold 20 meetings, with the average being eight sessions per year with length of meetings from 30 minutes to three days, with the average being 2.45 hours. There is no norm, but one can safely say that any meeting as important as a school board that lasts a mere 30 minutes is frivolous, while one that last for six hours has probably delved too deep into the operational management of the school.

It is here that the role of the chair is critical, for it is the chair who guides and summarises discussions, who encourages every member to speak, who maintains focus on the issue in hand and who, at the appropriate time, brings the matter to a conclusion. The chair, more than any other board member, must be fully cognisant on all issues facing the school, must be conscious of any personal agendas that board members may bring to the meeting, must be the voice of the board in the community, including being supportive of the head in public, while being prepared to coach, criticise and cajole in private.

My personal experience from a range of International schools is that one or two meetings a term is sufficient for the board to meet its obligations, and that these meetings should take in the region of two to two-and-a-half hours, depending on the complexity of the agenda, and the extent to which members have prepared themselves for the meeting.

Too many cooks may spoil the broth, but too few and the broth may not appear. The analogy may not be too precise, but the idea is as applicable to boards as it is to cooks. There is no 'perfect' number for a board, as it depends primarily on the constitution. The CIS survey shows board membership ranging from three to 28; my belief is that a board of six to nine is appropriate for most schools, together with the ability to co-opt additional non-voting members for specific projects such as a major construction programme.

The role of the board is not only to provide strategic guidance and support to the head, but also to provide access for the head, whose needs will change over time, to a range of specialist expertise. This is where committees become an integral part of the structure, as they enable the school to benefit from the wider range of expertise from the whole school community, whether they are parents, alumni or professionals in the community working on a *pro bono* basis. A subsequent chapter in this book explains in detail the options available through a committee structure, to which I would add a caveat: there is a danger that a committee is perceived to be a forum for deliberation rather than action. There are occasions when a 'task force' is a more appropriate description as this is more often than not perceived to imply responsiveness and action. While a case can be argued for ongoing standing committees in areas such as finance, it is probable that a task force with the remit to review, report and recommend on a specific issue is the more frequent requirement. I caution against blind acceptance of any committee structure, and the purpose of each committee and task force should be reviewed as part of the annual board appraisal process. Despite what may appear as a somewhat negative approach to committees, they do provide a valuable function in identifying people prepared to dedicate time to the school, and hence a pipeline of candidates for future board positions.

Let me now take the nine constituents of an effective board given earlier and review each in a little more detail.

Work together by consensus without being afraid to debate contentious issues

Boards, like schools, work best in a collegial atmosphere, but this allows on occasions the dangerous principle of 'management-by-doing-nothing' to predominate when contentious issues arise. Denial of a problem is not an effective means of solving the problem, with the likely consequence that the issue may spiral out of control. The fear of giving offence, the fear of the consequences or uncertainty of one's position or role are the common reasons for denial. This is an area where effective, structured board training can help ensure that contentious issues are raised, followed by a healthy debate and conclusion. Debate does not negate the collegial culture of a board; denial does.

Leave any personal agendas outside the boardroom door

Nothing, but nothing, is more destructive of board effectiveness than a member pursuing his or her personal agenda without consideration for the views of others or the good of the school. We have all, I am sure, heard horror stories similar to that of the excellent teacher whose contract was not renewed because a board member's child was reprimanded in class, or of a head who was summarily fired because he would not allow a board member's child to be placed in a class above his year group. *Caveat emptor!*

Are responsive to the views of others and leave any disagreements within the confines of the meeting

This is closely related to our first point but sufficiently important to warrant a section on its own. Respect for the views of others is not just good manners, it is essential for an open debate and conclusion on the issue. Disagreements are healthy but collective responsibility for board decisions, whatever one's personal view, is critical for effective management. If an individual board member feels sufficiently strongly against a board position, they have a clear option: resign.

Leave the management of the school to those entrusted with its task

This is the hardest task of all, and one which gives rise to the most angst amongst heads. The task of the board is to provide strategic direction, guide and evaluate the head of school and approve budgets. The day-to-day management of the school is the responsibility of the head assisted by the school senior management team. It can be useful to create a matrix of scenarios, ranging from issues that are clearly under the remit of the board, through those on which the board should be consulted to those that are clearly under the remit of the head. Micromanagement by boards can become especially prevalent during periods of transition where the outgoing head, despite the best will in the world, is likely to be distracted by the challenges of his new position to the detriment of the current school. The board can and on occasions should get directly involved in management under these circumstances but must then stand back and let the incoming head run the show. If they do not, they run the serious risk of a frustrated head and a contentious board.

Maintain strict confidentiality of all discussions

Easy to say, but sometimes difficult to achieve. Unless there is complete confidentiality of board discussions, contentious issues will not be raised let alone debated. Confidentiality does, however, run contrary to the principle of transparency, which is essential for both ownership and accountability. The balance is fine and, while board decisions should be in the public domain, the discussions behind them should not. How often have you heard board issues being discussed in the local Starbucks the following day?

Maintain a sense of proportion and a sense of humour

'Out of little acorns great oaks grow' is as applicable to small issues as it is to great ideas. Keep that sense of proportion and the use of light humour can effectively defuse tension at home, at work or in the school boardroom. And finally: take what you do seriously but never take yourself too seriously.

Set objectives for the board and evaluate themselves against those objectives

We require objective setting and evaluation for our staff; it is right and proper that we should do so for ourselves. Setting objectives helps to avoid the possibility of falling into micromanagement, while evaluation should be an examination as to how effectively the board has worked as a team against those objectives. I also believe that it is important for each individual board member to stand back and evaluate their own performance as a member of that team: have they left personal agendas behind; have they contributed fully to the debate; have they come to meetings fully prepared; have they maintained confidentiality; in sum, have they played an effective role in the performance of the board.

Retain a clear focus on their objective to improve the learning environment for students

Here we come full circle: unless the activities of the board have contributed to an improved learning environment, they have wasted their time, done a disservice to the students, their parents and the school community and should make way for others who will hold to this noble objective.

Conclusion

We all start our time as amateurs when appointed to boards, regardless of the professionalism we may practice in our daily lives. But for the board, not the individual, to be a *tour-de-force* requires training, commitment to a set of ideals and practices and, above all, the recognition that the contribution that we make towards improving the learning environment is the greatest legacy that we can leave to the school and future generations.

Chapter Three

The board, strategic planning,
and the strategic plan

It is already clear from the opening chapters that the board's primary role is to safeguard the school's future, which is another way of saying 'to think and act strategically'. It is remarkable that while many boards and school administrators often repeat the mantra 'the board must be strategic', not so many have a clear idea what this means in practice, and in particular what boards must do to give it effective meaning. This chapter therefore outlines the board's role in strategic planning and its relationship to the strategic plan. In doing so, it also generates the framework within which all other board activities and responsibilities should be viewed.

Firstly, let us be sure what the terms 'strategic planning' and 'strategic plan' actually mean, how they differ from operational planning and plans, and what the implications are for International schools, their boards, and their administrators.

Much has been written on this subject, including an article and a practical guide by two of this book's contributors, but it is sufficient for our immediate purpose to say that strategic planning is a systematic method to assess how the world will change, how the school will be affected, and to plan how the school should respond in order to deliver its mission and meet its objectives.

In the first analytical phase, it looks closely at what the school is, what it intends to be, what its current situation is, and what opportunities and challenges the future will bring.

In the second development phase, it identifies the handful of key strategies that will enable the school to grasp the opportunities and handle the challenges. This is the strategic plan, which acts as the template and guide for everything the school will do in the future.

In the third implementation phase, a cascade of more detailed plans for the immediate and medium-term future are developed and implemented.

Two critical points arise here, one to do with involvement, the other to do with obsolescence. In both cases, there are opportunities and potential pitfalls in equal measure.

A feature of many International schools that distinguishes them from other types of independent school is the transient nature of its community of students, parents, faculty, administrators and board members, which puts particular strain on maintaining continuity, institutional knowledge and a shared sense of purpose. Anything which promotes common understanding and vision must therefore be viewed positively. The strategic planning process presents a wonderful opportunity to involve all the school's stakeholders in shaping the school's future, which has the dual benefit of both aligning all sections of the community in a common purpose and way forward, and in gaining the widest and most credible range of insights into the future (which may be quite different to those of the leadership!). Conversely, if the process ignores the stakeholders, not only is it likely that the school's future is predicated on one narrow view, but those who will be charged with implementing the resulting plan are highly unlikely to share that view and will have little understanding or sense of ownership, and whether by intent, indifference or ignorance, have the potential to sabotage the plan and programme it for failure before it starts.

The second point arises from a common perception that any planning beyond the immediately obvious is a complete waste of time and effort: the world changes so much and so quickly that today's plans are obsolete before the ink is dry. This is a common experience if the plans are based on the circumstances and assumptions of the day, and gives a very strong clue to what strategic planning is not: it is <u>not</u> a longer-term version of operational planning!

Successful strategic planning deals with the issue of obsolescence in two ways. Firstly, during the development phase it deliberately sets out to look beyond the immediate horizon, and identify trends and events that do not follow the patterns of the immediate past (which is how most operational planning is developed). Secondly, it puts a system in place to review regularly the effectiveness of the strategies, to test the continuing validity of the key assumptions, to continue to look over the horizon, and to adjust strategies if necessary. This systematic and regular review, always questioning, probing and testing, and acting decisively when it is clear that something significant has changed, is what keeps the plan live and robust, and prevents it from becoming 'obsolete before the ink is dry'.

Using the techniques of operational planning to develop a strategic plan can happen in any organisation, and we believe arises from the intense pressure that senior executives and school administrators alike feel to deliver operational excellence and immediate results. Excellence and good results are vitally important, of course, but thinking strategically requires a different mindset, and needs time to be set aside, because it is impossible to think strategically and operationally at the same time. When so many urgent day-to-day issues are jostling for attention, it takes real will and determination not to slide back into an operational mode!

So what is the board's role in all this?

Essentially, the board exists to ensure that a 'strategic mindset' is continuously at work, searching the future for reassurance that the current direction is still correct, or more importantly for signs that something needs to change, because the earlier those signs can be detected, the more time the school has to plan for and adjust to the new circumstance with the minimum of disruption and tension. The board's role here is a vital support to the senior administration and to the head of school in particular, because we demand that those senior administrative positions think strategically and plan for the long term, and at the same time handle the clamour, urgency and immediacy of day-to-day operations.

As we scan the strategic planning process, we can see where the board plays its part in both establishing a meaningful and vibrant strategic plan, and how it then uses the plan as the template for its activities through the school year.

First of all, of course, something, or someone, has to trigger the process. In our view, that can only be the school's leadership: as with any major project, if it does not start at the top, it does not start at all ! Only those in authority can both allocate the resources and convey the message that this is a necessary exercise that has their full support and commitment. Earlier, we said that a feature of many International schools that sets them apart from other types of independent school is the transient nature of its stakeholders; another highly relevant feature that sets them apart is the degree to which leadership is jointly exercised by the board chair and head of school. Indeed, the degree to which they operate in harmony largely determines how smoothly and successfully the school operates. The board chair therefore has a key role with the head of school in deciding to launch the strategic planning process, and selecting the key players who will run it.

The board itself will participate in the analytical phase as stakeholders. It will also supply key members of the task force that sifts through the community's responses and background information, arrives at the handful of key activities that are critical to the school's future, and assigns cost, resources, timing and responsibility for them.

At this point, the board assumes its primary and perhaps most critical role. It must now satisfy itself that the plan addresses all the elements for which it is accountable; that the actions are absolutely necessary for the future of the school; and that they can be achieved with the available resources of people, cash and time. The board is essentially committing the school to a particular path for the next few years, so it must be convinced that the plan both meets the school's objectives and is realistic in its demands on time, funds and people's effort, bearing in mind that all along the school has to operate smoothly day-to-day as well!

Once the board formally accepts the plan, it should very publicly communicate it to all stakeholders and invite the community to celebrate the achievement. This not only acknowledges the efforts and contributions that everybody has made, but signals the direction and key actions that the school is adopting, and for which the board and senior administration are taking responsibility. This not only brings clarity and removes ambiguity, but provides a quick and straightforward mechanism for inducting new stakeholders as they enter the community.

The board is not only accepting the plan on behalf of the community and the school's employees. The plan and its regular review now becomes the template for the board's own activities. Everything the board does should either ensure that the plan stays live and robust, or supports an activity directly connected to the plan, both of which will translate into the way the board sets its goals and works with administrators and other stakeholders through its committee structure.

The outcome of the strategic planning process is exciting and tremendously reassuring, but it is also long, intense and arduous. However, once in place, and provided it is kept up-to-date and live through regular review, it ensures that the board clearly understands and stays focused on its role of ensuring that the school is delivering its mission, and that the school's future is safe-guarded. This focus also ensures that the board does not stray into operational matters other than to assure itself that the school's values are being maintained and that the school's day-to-day activity is directly linked to its strategic direction and objectives.

Bibliography

Hodgson/Chuck (2003) *Strategic Planning in International schools.* ECIS/CIS.

Hodgson/Chuck (April 2004) Strategic planning: a practical approach for International schools, *International schools Journal*, Vol XXIII No 2.

Chapter Four

The board and operations

The opening chapters focused strongly on the board's strategic role, and mentioned several times that the board must not involve itself in operational matters. Does this therefore mean that the board has no interest and no role in the day-to-day running of the school?

Indeed it does not! However, what different people believe should be the board's role and interest is perhaps the source of more friction and conflict in International school governance than any other. This may occur between the board and the head of school, the board and faculty, the board and parents, or even between board members themselves. It is therefore fundamentally vital that the board's role is very clearly defined, that board members themselves thoroughly understand and accept it, and that it is clearly and repeatedly communicated to the community at large.

The board's role

It is absolutely clear that irrespective of the type of ownership, the head of school is charged with the responsibility to establish an administrative and departmental structure to develop and implement the curriculum, and assure the smooth running of the school, within the school's stated values and principles.

The board's role is focused very clearly on satisfying itself, and thereby the person, body or community that it represents, that two criteria are being met: firstly, that the school is doing what it is supposed to do ('delivering its Mission'); secondly, that it is doing so according to its stated behavioural values and educational principles. **It is both implicit and explicit that the board does not itself carry out the delivery of the Mission.**

So given these very distinct and logical roles, why can there be such confusion and friction?

Different expectations

Realistically, few people outside the immediate running of the school will have much grasp of governance or feel that it impinges on their lives. For the majority, the first time they come into contact with it is during a crisis that affects them, their children or, in the case of faculty, their jobs. Then their real expectations emerge, profusely coloured by the emotion of the moment and the outcome they so desperately crave. (This is partly the reason for this book!)

Furthermore, even well-engaged and well-informed people are likely to have expectations that are derived from their past experience and, when they come from so many different education systems, it is hardly surprising that they expect different things and instinctively expect the school to behave and react as they were used to 'back home'.

As if that were not enough, there is also the feature of International schools that compounds every problem and complicates every communication: turnover. This is not just the absence of the familiarity that comes with a settled existence; people who are in one place for two or three years and then move on are hardly likely to take a great interest in how the school will evolve over the next five or 10 years. They are only interested in what the school will do for them and their children (and to be fair, what they can do for the school) while they are there. This necessarily focuses their entire attention on the day-to-day. If and when something happens that, for example, brings them into conflict with the school, they may try to enlist the support of 'their' representatives, *ie* board members, instinctively believing that the board is as involved in the here and now as everyone else!

In addition, in any educational system, there can be a reluctance to take a grievance directly to its source, however strenuously a head or an administration stress that this is the right thing to do. This may be anxiety about confronting 'the experts', a sense of being a lone voice against the system, a worry that there will be repercussions for the child, or a belief that the school will simply close ranks to defend its position. Whatever it is, there seems to be a greater comfort in lobbying the board to fight the battle on their behalf in the belief that the board has the duty, the power and the clout to get things done.

If trustees are drawn from the parent community, either by election or by appointment, this basic misunderstanding may be carried into the board itself. Indeed, some parents may join the board with the specific intent to influence the running of the school. If this is not carefully and comprehensively confronted before and after election or appointment, the seeds will be sown for discord in the board itself, and between the board and all the other stakeholders.

Heads of school, by their nature, are professionals who know and understand good governance. They know perhaps better than anyone how an effective board can support them but also how destructive a dysfunctional board can be. They know that they have a duty to help educate board members in good governance. However, for those who have to do this without help or support, one may understand if they become tired of trying to educate a virtually new board every year, finding it easier and more time-efficient simply to neutralise them. Under these circumstances, the seeds of discord will flourish unless there are strong efforts to root them out.

What can be done about it?

The key to any solution, wherever confusion or discord arises, lies in clearly defined policy, thorough and intensive training, and continuous communication, with the objective of maintaining the continuity of institutional knowledge.

The board and head of school

The relationship between the board and head of school is so critical that a separate chapter is devoted to it. Among other things it talks about the separation of duties and the ways in which the head and the board can help, support and work with each other for the benefit of the school. However, as far as the board's monitoring role is concerned, the message can be summarised in one statement: a school where the head helps and encourages the board to verify the school's performance, and acts when short comings are noted, will find its communications with parents and the community carry much more weight, and its board able to voice its support much more credibly and authoritatively.

The board itself

Alongside this relationship the board itself must be internally of one mind and at peace with itself. The head of school, the board chair, the chair of the trustees' committee (if such a body exists) all have a vital role to play in educating new members in their roles and responsibilities, ensuring a common understanding. The opening chapters discussed the characteristics that make a good trustee, and how to look for potential trustees with these attributes and avoid those who have their own agendas or conflicting ideas. This can be problematic when trustees are elected from the parent body, where there is the greatest potential for these issues to surface. This puts extra responsibility on the body organising the election or appointment system (normally a nominating or trustees' committee) to accept only nominations of people who endorse and agree to abide by the board's role.

The board and faculty

The relationship between board and faculty is necessarily less close than with other parts of the school community as faculty is accountable to the head of school through the administration structure. However, when the relationship between board and administration is sound, faculty can work routinely and very successfully with board members to demonstrate how and to what extent they are measuring progress and driving improvements. If the role of the board in this situation is clear to both board members and faculty, it will also be clear that a well-informed and knowledgeable board can help the school to progress, not only by providing an objective sounding board, but also by verifying what the community is hearing from its normal sources. Confident schools will welcome this extra mechanism to show how well they are doing, to identify where they can improve, and to confirm that they are continuously in touch with and delivering what their communities expect.

The board and parents

We have noted that in International schools, the greatest potential for misunderstanding the board's monitoring role lies with parents, yet this is precisely the section of the community whose support the school needs most. It is therefore in the school's best interest to do its very best to ensure that parents understand exactly what the board's responsibilities are; unfortunately, successful communication on this subject is fraught with difficulty. Even the most receptive parents will struggle to absorb the entire cascade of communications that accompany a normal working week. Matters of policy and interpretation rarely register on the average family radar screen until a crisis occurs, and even then only if it directly affects them or their children.

In the final analysis, even when the head and board communicate regularly and clearly about such matters, it will only really register when a problem arises, a board member is approached to 'do something about it', and the board member has to explain patiently and clearly what their role is and to whom they will redirect the aggrieved parent.

How can the board best conduct its responsibility?

Even though the board's primary role is strategic and to hold the school in trust for future generations, it must not forget its responsibility to the current generation of students and parents to monitor the school's performance and to verify that the school is acting according to its principles.

There are two aspects for the board to consider: the framework that allows it to measure the school's performance and progress, and the mechanism by which it can do this efficiently and effectively.

The framework will start with the school's statements of purpose and values (Mission and Values statement) and its policies. These are the basic statements that guide everything the school does and ensure it lives according to its values and principles. The framework continues with its procedures, which document how things will be done and the goals which it sets itself each year. This combination now allows the board to understand what the school aims to achieve and how it can judge whether it is achieving it. Note that the school itself sets its operational goals. All the board has to do is to satisfy itself that these goals are consistent with the school's strategic direction, to understand how progress towards these goals will be measured, and invite the school to demonstrate regularly what progress is being made towards them.

It is worth repeating that the board has no role in conducting operations; it only has to know enough to understand them, and to verify that they are being conducted properly.

There are various mechanisms that a board can employ to fulfil this role. The most common and probably the most efficient (when well run) is a committee structure. The role and function of committees are examined closely in Chapter 5, but in summary, they examine the key elements of the school's activities and look both at the strategic requirements (as generated in the strategic planning process) and the oversight of operations. Thus a finance committee will concern itself with both the next year's enrolment and budget, and the long-term financial planning necessary to support the schools' strategic objectives. An education committee will examine both the school's current academic performance and plans, and what must happen to achieve the school's strategic target for, say, IB accreditation within five years.

It is of course likely that board members may supply more active help and expertise in finance than in education, but the monitoring and verification role that the board performs on behalf of the community is equally vital in both. If used and guided wisely, it will be of immense help and support to the head of school and his administration.

Chapter Five

The board and its committees

As we have seen, the board has two key roles: to safeguard the school's future for the following generations of students; and to assure the community that the school is operating within its values and performing to the community's needs and expectations.

These are grand ideals whose fine words give no clue to the difficulty of putting them into practice! This chapter therefore concentrates on the mechanisms available to those boards that have a broad remit to both monitor the performance of the school and to safeguard and plan for its future.

It is clear that some form of organisational structure will be needed to ensure that the board's duties are fully discharged and that board members are all involved and their time effectively used. There are various ways that different boards achieve this but most fall within a classical 'committee' structure in which the key elements of the school for which the board is accountable are each assigned to a committee that works continuously and reports regularly to the full board. These committees may be permanent or 'standing', or they may be formed to carry out a specific task with a defined beginning and end. For the sake of clarity and consistency, we shall use the term 'committee' for a standing or permanent body, and the term 'task force' for a time-limited body with a defined task.

How many should there be and what subjects do they address?

The committees are the working groups that enable the board to function, so there must be enough to cover the key strategic subjects but, with time and energy at a premium, no more than absolutely necessary to carry out the board's duties. The number of committees is therefore directly related to the board's primary responsibilities and duties.

If a school defines its board's duties as, for example, ensuring a strong robust educational program, establishing the school's policies, ensuring a strong financial position, maintaining adequate facilities, and selecting and evaluating the head of school, its committee and task force structure would reflect exactly these duties.

However, this would not in itself be enough for a strong strategic board. There are two other vital functions that must be addressed and for which well-designed committees are an effective mechanism.

The first function maintains the board's health, vigour and effectiveness through a committee variously known as the trustees' committee, governance committee or board development committee. Whatever it is called, it has a broad remit that goes far beyond the role of the traditional nominating committee. Amongst other things, it ensures that:

- the board is populated with the best and most effective people (the function of the traditional nominating committee);

- new board members are welcomed and become effective quickly;
- all board members are thoroughly trained;
- the board conducts a rigorous annual self-evaluation and acts on the outcome;
- the board maintains continuous and effective communication with its community;
- the board safeguards, updates and passes on its institutional knowledge and experience.

Many international communities, schools and boards are in such a constant state of turnover and new faces that achieving these objectives is both vital and a major challenge to consistent and effective governance. Furthermore, and as noted in other chapters, one of the head's many duties is to educate new board members. In this respect, a good trustees' committee can make a massive contribution, not just to helping to bring and keep board members up to speed, but also to lightening the load on the shoulders of the head of school. It is no surprise that many prominent names in International education believe this committee to be 'first among equals' in terms of its contribution to good governance.

The *NAIS Trustee Handbook* has a particularly good chapter on the function and duties of this committee.

The second extra committee is truly 'future-oriented'. It continuously 'scans' the school's external environment for the earliest possible indication of new opportunities or threats. In fact, this activity is the sole function of the boards of certain proprietor schools, who operate like the governing councils of national independent schools by concerning themselves only with such purely strategic issues. However, whether it is the sole activity of the board or the function of one of its committees, the purpose is clear: to give the school the maximum time and chance to evaluate the opportunity or threat and to plan how to respond to it. It really is the school's 'early warning system', and with acknowledgment to a certain UK advertising slogan in the 1950s: every school should have one!

In addition, a school may have a separate strategic monitoring committee that concerns itself with the monitoring and review of its strategic plan, or it may devolve this vital function to its individual committees, but either way there must be a mechanism by which the board ensures that the strategic plan is being regularly monitored, reviewed and updated.

In keeping with its strategic remit, the board should not have committees to cover operational matters such as recruitment or marketing unless there is a strong strategic element which the board needs to address. In such a case, it is more likely that the board will establish a task force to address the matter in detail, make a recommendation, and then disband.

In summary, a medium-sized to large school would expect to have committees covering education, finance, facilities (also called buildings and grounds), governance, policy, and external environment.

What is their function?

A committee has two functions. For the element for which it is responsible, it has a strategic role in which it either participates in or tracks the actions identified in the strategic plan and recommends changes should circumstances demand, and a monitoring role in which it enables the board to re-assure itself and the community that the school is delivering its Mission. These two roles directly determine the committee's goals, ensuring it stays focused on what is necessary and important, and does not become side-tracked by irrelevant or trivial matters, or matters which are not the committee's concern.

The strategic function is the means by which the school ensures its strategic plan is being properly and fully implemented and, as importantly, is kept up-to-date, live, and responsive to changing circumstances. The use of the committee structure to do this is an efficient and effective means to keep board members, administrators and other interested members of the community focused on the strategic development of the school.

The monitoring role that committees must fulfil can be fraught with difficulty, so we will spend some time to examine it in detail; to understand how committee members can work effectively together while avoiding some of the more common pitfalls.

At the outset, two key statements must be stressed: firstly, a committee is neither a substitute for, nor a duplication of, the administration's responsibility for managing day-to-day operations; secondly, a committee must never be tempted to assume a problem-solving role in operational matters. A committee's interest in the day-to-day running of the school is confined to whether the school is operating within its values and whether the outcome is meeting the community's requirements and expectations. This obviously requires that committee members have knowledge and understanding of operations, and the means by which progress is measured, but this must never be confused with operating responsibility.

It is vital that board members and administrators clearly understand their own and each other's roles and responsibilities in this respect to ensure they work harmoniously together. The absence of this mutual understanding is perhaps the main source of friction between board members and administrators to the detriment of both groups and of the school as a whole.

Sadly, too many administrators instinctively see a committee's monitoring role either as an unwarranted interference or as an unwelcome inspection to be limited and obstructed as far as possible. Unfortunately, this just serves to reinforce the suspicion that there is something to hide! If administrators are open and honest, and board members show appropriate respect and treat the sometimes sensitive information with care, both groups will find that the committees provide an efficient, effective and objective system to demonstrate how the school is striving to meet the community's requirements, and to identify and facilitate ways to improve.

The education committee is particularly susceptible to this problem. Administrators can feel that they are educational professionals who can and should be trusted to deliver the educational mission and to keep the community informed and that the committee, by its nature, has only limited understanding of education and therefore brings little of value. However, this approach can never avoid the suspicion that 'they only tell us what they want to tell us'. It does not recognise that even if board members are not professional educators, they represent a community that knows what it wants, with a duty to check that the delivery is meeting requirements and expectations. It is far better and much more constructive for the experts to help board members understand what constitutes 'good education', and then demonstrate what is happening to achieve it. This not only helps administrators maintain clarity and focus in their own educational thinking but enables board members to contribute fully and to be credible in their public support for the school.

Who should serve on committees?

Generally committees will consist of a mix of board members, administrators and others with specific interest and expertise. This approach has a number of positive effects: it ensures that all board members are involved and utilised, that administrators are fully involved in strategic matters, and that others outside the board and administration can be involved and contribute their particular knowledge and experience. In addition, it fosters a close working relationship between board members and administrators which is both positive for the school, generating confidence and support from the wider community.

Each committee will be chaired by a board member, with at least one other board member participating and able to take the chair if necessary. The board chair and head of school will be *ex officio* members of all committees, but time constraints will normally restrict their attendance to those committees where their presence is particularly needed. The head of school, in consultation with the committee chair, will normally assign the administrators who will serve on each committee. The committee chair will decide on any necessary additional members, recognising that the optimum committee size is between six and eight members, and that any extra people must abide by the rules of confidentiality that govern board members themselves.

Sometimes an issue arises that requires knowledge or expertise not available within the regular members, in which case the chair can co-opt someone to attend while that particular issue is being considered.

How often should committees meet?

As with board meetings, the meeting frequency must reflect the time commitment of members and the work that has to be covered. Committee work is generally continuous but committees do need to meet regularly to review progress, discuss issues and draw up reports and recommendations for the board. Generally committees can operate effectively when they meet six to eight times per school year. Ideally, a calendar with all board and committee meetings should be drawn up at the beginning of the school year to ensure that participants can block all relevant dates in their diaries, that dates do not clash with each other or important events, and that meetings fit into logical reporting sequences (*eg* a finance committee meeting to finalise next year's budget would logically take place two to three weeks before the budget is presented to the board).

Goal-setting and reporting to the board

The committees exist to enable the board as a whole to carry out its strategic and monitoring duties. Each committee will therefore report its particular strategic and monitoring activities. The best way for this to happen is that at the beginning of the school year each committee establishes its goals for the year, which the board then considers and approves. Each committee then reports against these goals at the regular board meetings. This approach ensures that committee meetings and board meetings alike concentrate purely on the matters in hand, do not go into too much detail, and do not drift into areas that do not concern them.

As with the board itself, committees should be careful in their goal-setting. In particular, they should set themselves real and appropriate goals, and not just vague statements of intent, such as 'to ensure the finances are sound' or 'to improve the quality of the mathematics teaching'. This is straightforward in areas like finance, for example, where an acceptable goal would be 'to present a balanced budget for the next school year at the February board meeting'. It can be much more tricky in areas like education where meaningful measures of quality and progress are harder to define. Here those with the expertise and experience must take the lead in helping the board to understand what constitutes high quality and how real progress can be measured.

The role of task forces

As already mentioned, there are occasions when a specific topic needs to be addressed, which has a defined beginning and end. In such cases, the board may appoint a task force, whose sole function is to address the topic in hand and disband when the task is complete. Just as with the standing committees, a task force may consist of board members, administrators and others with the appropriate knowledge and expertise to enable the best result to be achieved.

Conclusion

For all but the smallest schools, the committee structure and approach is the most effective and efficient way for a board to discharge its duties. At the same time it allows wider participation from the community in the governance of the school and close cooperation between the administrative and governing functions. It is important that all participants understand and accept their own and each other's roles and responsibilities to ensure that all sections work harmoniously and constructively together, for the good of the school and for those for whom the school ultimately exists – its students.

Bibliography

DeKuyper, Mary Hundley (1998) *Trustee Handbook – A guide to Effective Governance for Independent School Boards*. Washington, DC: NAIS.

Chapter Six

The board and the head of school

This chapter attempts to catalogue suggestions for both the heads of schools and their governing boards as they work together in partnership for the improvement of learning in their schools. These suggestions need to be analysed to determine if they are applicable to any individual school or non-profit organisation. There are now thousands of schools offering international education programmes, and millions of boards associated with non-profit organisations.

Each institution has its own needs. However, most of my observations will relate to my experience as a director, principal and board member of four International schools in addition to serving as an associate superintendent in a major urban school district. I have worked with appointed and elected boards as well as boards with a mix of appointed and elected members. In my 40 years of working with boards (or serving as a board member), the least effective model were totally elected untrained parent boards. Even with training, many parent board members have difficulty in separating the needs of their family from those of the school. All models have enjoyed degrees of success.

The basic assumption for this chapter is that the board is the guardian of the school's mission. It ensures that the mission remains relevant to the needs of the school community being served and monitors the success of the school in fulfiling this mission. It has a key role in strategic planning, budget development and approval, along with policy formulation and adoption. It is also engaged in selecting, supporting, nurturing and evaluating their head of school.

Bill Powell characterises the main work of the board as 'thinking, considering, evaluating, planning and serving as a critical friend to the head of school'. They need to work together to nurture a special relationship with each other, while trusting the good intentions of each other. They must assume each other's integrity. This is the theme of a complementary ECIS book in this series (2001) by Powell, Bowley, and Schoppert, *School Board Governance and Training*. This excellent publication in the Effective International schools Series also offers advice on how to improve relationships when conflicts arise. Head-board conflicts seldom arise when they both realise that their power needs to be shared and used to motivate and effect change in the school. This realisation often comes about when the head and board know each other well enough to be able to predict and appreciate each other's opinions and reactions to situations as they arise. To achieve this, the head (and the board chair) must supply the 'social glue' that helps the board to be a cohesive and productive group.

What needs to be remembered is that most board members have not been systematically prepared for their roles. They usually include a collection of 'successful' individuals who may not perform well as a group. However they sincerely desire to be effective board members. "The first lesson to be learned," Drucker advised, "is that non-profits need clear and functioning governance structure. They have to take their governance seriously, and they have to work hard on it" (1990). When heads are well prepared for their roles, they must be active catalysts in helping board members learn in an ongoing manner, in addition to any formal board-head training program.

Building the partnership

The suggestions that follow are based on the assumption that the board and the head wish to work together to create a partnership based on mutual support and trust. In this partnership, International school board members often acknowledge the head as their *de facto* leader. The head, engaged full time in the school, is viewed as being experienced in governance and as an expert in education. This mutual dependence is a unique relationship in which the board and head rely on each other to exchange information and support that enables them to perform their respective roles more effectively (Blau, 1986). This assumption requires that the head and board members can function as critics, friends, counsellors and confidants. Boards should be encouraged to perceive their head as a teacher, leader, employee, colleague and advisor (Chait, Holland and Taylor, 1993). This concept may seem idealistic to some, knowing that a successful partnership will depend on honest communication and an open acknowledgement of interdependence.

Drucker (1990) also supported this concept when he wrote that:

> Non-profits waste uncounted hours debating who is superior and who is subordinate – board or executive officer. The answer is that they must be colleagues. Each has a different part, but together they share the play. Their tasks are complementary. Thus, each has to ask, what do I owe the other? Not – as board and executive officers still tend to do – what does the other owe me?

It is essential, however, in this pivotal partnership or 'exchange relationship', that the head (or head and chair) must accept the ongoing obligation of regular board development and training. CIS accreditation standards also ensure that appropriate training exists for both the board and head of CIS accredited schools.

This need for training is particularly important in International schools where there tends to be a high turnover of both heads and board members. However, one of our goals must be to create conditions that promote more continuity of governing boards and school administrators in each school, if optimal learning in these schools is to take place! We know that continuity is significantly enhanced when an effective partnership exists.

Obviously this partnership can get off to a good start when the board selects a head who shares their vision and is sincerely committed to the mission of the school. This process best includes a process where the board considers input from staff, parents and students in making their selection. In addition, the prospective head must be able to understand the selection criteria and the approach to governance envisioned by the board before accepting any offer that may follow.

Where the goals and mission are not already defined and widely agreed upon, the board must expect and support the leadership of the new head in gaining board, community and staff support for a school mission statement. Organisations are built on the unification of people around values (Greenfield, 1991).

In analysing the board-head partnership, most board members believe that the head usually occupies the more powerful position in the relationship. The head has more time, expertise and information to offer, and therefore more influence over board agenda, meetings and decision-making processes. Most boards want to support their head. It is hoped that their support is not based upon their insecurity or ignorance about the issues being faced! This disengagement should be avoided, as heads also need sources of objective advice and critical feedback, which they may not be receiving from faculty, subordinates and parents. Heads have a deeply vested, personal interest in fostering boards that are engaged. This engagement will lead to a deeper understanding of their role as board members, a greater appreciation of the head's role and circumstances, and a heightened commitment to the mission of the school.

Board-head training framework: some guidelines

1. Heads must convince board leaders to make board-head training and annual goal-setting a priority while demonstrating that they are also learners seeking new knowledge and skills.

2. Heads may need to propose the agenda for training workshops, but should always insist that the board chair chairs the sessions.

3. Training workshops should be used to clarify roles, responsibilities and relationships, helping board members to resist pressures from parents to meddle in management, personnel issues, student discipline, business affairs, *etc*. The resulting protocol should be in writing, but exercised in a collaborative manner with mutual input as appropriate.

4. Board training workshops should be used to focus on the building blocks of good governance: board meetings, agenda development, board committees, board communication to parents and staff, *etc*.

5. Both the board and the heads should agree upon the procedures and criteria by which their effectiveness is to be evaluated. This should be a continuous process. A board committee should meet periodically with the head for a full and frank discussion of the head's performance, in addition to suggestions from the head on how the board-head partnership can be enhanced. Hawley's research also showed longer head tenure when there was a formal evaluation process in place.

6. Board must see continuing professional development as a sound investment (Malpass, 1994).

Guiding principles for a positive partnership

These suggestions are not prioritised, but can be considered as to their relevancy for each school:

General suggestions:

a) All board members are to be shown equal status by the head and staff.

b) All board members should know the school and its mission well, with the head orchestrating their growing understanding of the key issues and programmes being implemented.

c) All board member visits to the school should be arranged via the head or management team members.

d) Any recommendations or complaints to board members should be shared directly with the head, and referred as necessary to the board on the advice of the head.

e) Heads should expect questions from the board regarding the operation of the schools, and accept them in a positive manner conducive to harmonious board-head relations and communication. The head can decide when and how to respond directly to these questions.

f) In some schools, Littleford suggests that up to 40% of the head's time is devoted to board-related activities. This is not likely the case in most International schools.

g) The head must deal openly, honestly and courteously with the board at all times (Malpass, 1994).

The role of the board chair in a successful partnership

Much is written about board-head relations, but the key to a successful partnership is often the relationship between the board chair and the head.

> Both of them need to make every effort to establish a solid and mutually supportive relationship of candour and trust, develop the capacity to be mutually critical, and learn from each other's feedback – all with the goal of making their work on behalf of the school most effective.
>
> *(DeKuyper, 1990)*

DeKuyper goes on to emphasise the essential elements in communication between the chair and the head:

> As a board chair you accept the responsibility of working with the head to resolve differences and problems throughout the head's tenure. As board chair you understand the importance of direct, mutually established goals to the head's annual evaluation and to the board's evaluation and your own as well. As board chair you understand that in accepting the leadership of the board, you make a serious commitment of mind and heart to the school and the head. You will work hard with your partner and share and enjoy the challenge.

Simply put, the head and the chair must sincerely want to be partners. However, their relationship must not be perceived as being so close, that it causes other board members to distance themselves from the chair or the head, which can create unwanted divisions within your governance team. The chair alone has little power, but needs to be a team-builder whose power comes from the ability to inspire and develop others.

Many writers talk about this partnership in sporting terms, where team-work is so important. DeKuyper compares the metaphors of a 'three-legged race', 'tennis doubles' and a baseball 'catcher-pitcher relationship.' All of those metaphors are applicable to some degree, but all three point to the basic need for both parties to consider each other as their 'coach, confidant, strategist, and friendly critic'.

Design of the partnership

Boards need a model for decision-making that demonstrates confidence in the head and staff to allow them to do their jobs without interference! In the NAIS Trustee Handbook, Mary Hundley DeKuyper (1998) suggests a design for a successful partnership. This model is consistent with success-ful practices in many International schools.

Policies	Time and Attention Graph
Strategies *Mission* *Survival* *Leadership* *Major*	Board's decision Head's advice
Partnership *Authorization* *Finance Policies* *Enrolment* *Employment Terms*	Shared decision: Board and Head
Operational *Admissions* *Staffing* *Program* *Systems*	Board's advice Head's decision

Above the diagonal line = allocation of board's time
Below the diagonal line = allocation of head's time

Communication, communication, communication

In my experience, the majority of problems or conflicts arise when there is not a free flow of information among all stakeholders. This is true for most organisations and institutions. Good governance depends upon enlightened decision-making. Board members need to be knowledgable about the school's needs if they are to make sound decisions to support the mission. They must receive relevant information in a timely and concise manner, with graphic presentations whenever they are helpful. The head and board should agree on the content and timing of an information system that is efficient and effective. As with parents and staff, anxiety develops when they are not kept informed. A free-flow approach to information sharing will significantly enhance board-head partnerships and their overall effectiveness. This means that the head is also personally accessible to board members within the limits of his or her time.

Role clarity: the governance 'game' needs rules

Much of this chapter has focused on promoting a genuine sense of partnership between the head and the board, thus creating a harmonious team where all members share a common vision and mission. But, in the proposed design of the partnership, there needs to be a clear understanding about the roles and responsibilities of each team member. The head must know clearly the limits of his roles and responsibilities for which he is accountable. But as Paul Houston states in his 2001 article: "accountability without authority is punishment." The board and head should monitor the success in fulfiling their mission, but the board must not get involved in specific management, personnel or curricular issues. They need to be concerned primarily about 'ends', not 'means'.

This division of responsibilities between head and board often comes apart when there is a high turnover of either heads or chairs. In International schools, we see many examples of board members inappropriately involved in personnel or curricular discussions, when the heads are changing too often. When this has happened, the new head needs to have the strength and courage to clarify his responsibilities and 'power' before accepting the position. However, younger heads may want the job 'too much' to make it a condition of their accepting a position. New chairs are also often concerned about having enough 'power' to make a difference in the success of a school during their time in office, and will choose to test the strength of the head. Long-term heads are often used to this situation and do not 'bend in the wind' easily!

Epilogue: policy development for role clarification

What is at the centre of an effective board-head partnership? In our International school communities, parents and staff are usually well aware if a productive partnership exists or not. Any sense of conflict in this relationship can have a damaging impact on the schools and the communities that they serve. When looking at the cause of these conflicts, the problem often rests with the lack of role clarity. This lack of clarity is often caused by the actions of the head.

We talk about the board's main role being budget, policy and the selection and support of the head. Heads say that the board is not to be concerned with operations, administration or personnel decisions. However, when we look at board meeting agendas, we often do not find many items dealing with policies or budget. Heads, who are largely responsible for preparing board agendas, promote role opacity by the issues that they present to the board for decision. When board and head share operational decision-making, and when too many board policies are operational in nature, the seeds are sown for conflict. When boards are forced to think and decide at the policy level, and not at the operational level, the number of policies needed will also be reduced. Some policies should also be developed to establish any limitations or boundaries within which the head should operate or decide. Boards and heads are likely to need training in policy development in order to create an approach to governance that allows the head the freedom to do his or her job, accompanied by an agreed upon accountability model for the anticipated results.

A strong commitment to a limited number of key policies and a revolving strategic plan (that actually *is* strategic!) seems to be the necessary foundation for the board and head working well together for the improvement of learning. The result should provide a level of role clarity where they are not consumed with the struggle as to who is the 'driver', *ie* who is in charge. Then, too, the boards have the opportunity to apply their wisdom and sound judgement in a satisfying manner within a harmonious and productive partnership. There is almost always a sincere desire for this partnership. We only need to create conditions that will help make it happen on a consistent basis.

Bibliography

Blau, P M (1986) *Exchange and Power in Social Life*. New Brunswick, NJ: Transaction.

Carver, J (1990) *Boards That Make a Difference: A New Design for Leadership in Non-Profit and Public Institutions*. San Fransisco, CA: Jossey-Bass Publishers.

Chait, R P, Holland, T P, and Taylor, B E (1993) *The Effective Board of Trustees*. Phoenix, AZ: Onyx Press.

DeKuyper, M H (1998) *Trustees Handbook*. Washington, DC: National Association of Independent Schools.

Drucker, P (1990) *Lessons for Successful Non-Profit Governance in Non-Profit Management and Leadership* 1 (1): pp.7-14.

Greenfield, W (1991) Toward a Theory of School Leadership, AERA paper. Chicago, April 3-7.

Hawley, D (1994) How Long do International School Heads Survive. *International schools Journal*, Vol. XIV, No.1, pp.8-21.

Houston, P Superintendents for the 21st Century: It's not Just a Job, It's a Calling. *The Kappa*, vol. 82, No. 6, pp.428-33.

Littleford, J (4/1999) *Leadership of Schools and the Longevity of School Heads*. Baton Rouge, LA: Littleford & Associates.

Malpass, D (1994) School Boards Need Management Training. *International schools Journal*, Vol. XIV, No. 1, pp.22-28.

Powell, W, Bowley, N, and Schoppert, G (2001) *School Board Governance and Training*. Suffolk, UK: John Catt Educational Ltd.

Chapter Seven

The board and managing conflict

Schools are institutions in which all stakeholders have high aspirations and unfulfilled expectations. Nowhere is this exemplified more than in International schools. As we have seen in earlier chapters, International schools are usually characterised by the richness of the ethnic, cultural, professional and experiential diversity of the school community. Ironically, this richness, which can bring so much good to the school community, can often be the source of so much unhappiness and conflict within the institution.

Each member of the community brings to the school his or her own world view, perspectives, norms and values. Each has expectations of the school and makes demands of the school. All of these are thrown into the melting pot of the school *milieu* and from it comes the finished product, the well-rounded, educated graduate whose 'potential has been achieved to the full'. Too often though, it appears that this 'melting pot' takes on the characteristics of a crucible: more time and effort is associated with the burning off of dross than the refining of the precious metal.

Conflict is a feature of social interaction. It has positive as well as negative effects depending upon the way it is managed. Coser (1956) states that "… no group can be entirely harmonious for it would then be devoid of process and structure." Groups require disharmony as well as harmony, dissociation as well as association. Conflicts between them are by no means altogether disruptive factors.

Littleford (1999), Schoppert, (2002) and Hawley (1994, 1995) all report that the turnover of heads, board chairs and board members as a result of unresolved conflict is a major problem facing the governance of International schools. As noted in other chapters, in many International schools consistent and effective governance does not occur due to the high rate of turnover of heads, chairs and board members.

Conflict at this level leads to educational dysfunction. A lowering of standards, both academic and behavioural, destroys the reputation of the school and individual staff and has a negative impact on marketing, student and staff recruitment and financial viability.

In this chapter we are concerned with conflict at the interface of management and governance.

The chair, board and head relationship

The chair, board members and head have unique and distinct roles and a major source of conflict arises when these roles become blurred. It is vital therefore for the success of a school that chair, board and head respect each other's roles and responsibilities and recognise the boundaries of their respective jurisdictions. Further, they should take formal and informal opportunities to increase their mutual understanding of these roles and responsibilities and of how their individual natures and personalities will harmonise in the effective governance of a school.

The board's role is two-fold: the development of strategic policy, and fiduciary trusteeship. The head's role is to carry out board policy at the operational level of the school. The chair's role is to ensure that board and head fulfil their respective roles efficiently and effectively.

The chair should act as the head's 'best friend'. An excellent working relationship between chair and head is vital for a healthy school. Usually the chair has a significant role to play in the appointment of the head. Once the head has been appointed, it is the chair's job to support him or her at all times.

The head is the chief executive officer of the school and must be allowed to act as such without interference of any kind from the chair or the board. Micromanagement, without invitation by the head, is totally unacceptable.

Remember that schools are not democratic; they never were and never will be because of the nature of the learning process. Someone has to teach and someone has to learn. That is the natural order of things. The head must be allowed to run the school as CEO within the terms of reference and policies of the board.

In the event that the head does not turn out to be the right person for the post, or things begin to go wrong operationally, then the chair will be the means by which remediation, training and support are provided to assist the head in meeting the board's requirements. If this fails, the chair will be the conduit by which the head's contract is terminated and a new head sourced.

In situations where the head is in post and a new chair is being sourced, it is essential that the head be involved in nominating a new chair. There is little point in a new chair being appointed if the head cannot work with that person. The head may as well seek for a new post at the earliest opportunity and avoid the heartache of a failed working relationship with the chair.

Chair and head must meet regularly to discuss the school. Preferably these meetings should be informal but both parties would be advised to keep notes of topics and individuals discussed and actions recommended.

Board members must observe the requirement to keep all board affairs confidential and to exercise discretion in what is said to parents, staff and the outside community. Members must control their desire or instinct to wish to appear all-powerful and all-knowing in front of other people!

Occasionally, but perhaps more often than we appreciate, board members allow themselves to be nominated for board membership with false motives. A board member is there to serve the needs of the school community as, and when, they are required. Sometimes, unfortunately, one finds board members seek nomination for selfish reasons stemming from a need to establish an identity and sense of status and importance within the parent community.

Bad news, gossip and innuendo travel fast and the further they travel and the longer it takes, the more likely they are to become distorted. Hence an unimportant or trivial event or comment reported injudiciously on the part of one individual at the level of governance and management can have far-reaching implications.

The nature of conflict in school governance/management

A conflict is an unresolved dispute. Dispute resolution is a normal part of everyday life for school managers. Students, staff and parents provide a ready source of daily problems and challenges which need to be resolved. The academic, professional, curricular, behavioural, logistical and financial concerns of the institution and disputes arising around and within school, keep management alert to the changing needs of the school community.

Unresolved daily challenges and concerns can become disputes. Disputes, in turn, become conflicts if not resolved speedily. In the majority of cases, all disputes and conflicts arising in school are resolved at the level of management. Only when situations cannot be resolved by management would the board, as a whole, be alerted and involved.

Conflict between board and head *may* arise as a result of incompetence on the part of the head. It may be the case that a head who comes with good credentials lacks the personal and professional skills required to carry out the requirements of the board in that particular school at that stage in its development. The chair will need to counsel the head on the matter, and suggest ways of assisting the head. If this meets with antagonism from the head, then it is in everyone's interest that the head be encouraged to move on as detailed in terms of the employment agreement existing between board and head.

The topic under consideration in this chapter and one which is of real concern to heads and boards alike, concerns those situations which arise all too frequently where the head is perfectly capable and competent but acquires a new board and chair during his or her tenure.

It is not uncommon for a head to be appointed by one board and find that three years later there is a new board, or for all practical purposes, effectively a new board and chair, who do not relate to the head or agree with his or her *modus operandi*. In many schools with a large transient population of students, the board members may change every two or three years. This is particularly so where board elections take place annually at an AGM. In these situations the head has no control over who is elected to the board and less control over who becomes chair.

Why things go wrong

Schools are an extreme form of social organisation where the stakes for success and failure are high. By the very nature of the learning process and the learning environment, the capacity for misunderstandings between student/student, student/teacher, teacher/teacher, teacher/administrator, parent/teacher and parent/administrator runs high.

Misunderstandings, misperceptions, disagreements, alternative views, different values, greed, ambition, personal aggrandisement, fear of failure and fear of rejection are but a few of the psychological issues loose within the school environment. Add to this the physiological changes associated with puberty and aging and there are preconditions for a series of challenges, concerns, disputes and conflicts which teachers and administrators grapple with on a daily basis and for which the majority of staff and administrators are prepared.

Conflicts at the highest levels of school organisation are not usually anticipated and hence, when they arise, the outcome is invariably extremely serious.

Conflicts can be precipitated in governance and management for a host of reasons but upon analysis, the distal cause of the conflict begins with one person and usually follows a route which can be represented by the following generalisation.

Every school has its share of disgruntled parents whether for real or imaginary reasons. It would be a rare school that doesn't have a dissatisfied member or two of staff, be they teachers or support staff. Boards too, can have a disgruntled member who has managed to be elected to the board but who does not have the correct motives for membership. Once an unhappy parent/staff member and an equally unhappy board member get together, it spells trouble for the head.

Parents can become emotional over a concern that their child is not receiving appropriate education or is being treated unfairly in some way. Usually, the matter is attended to at the most appropriate level within the organisation, which is usually by the teacher. If the parent is reasonable and satisfaction has been achieved by a meeting, then the matter will be concluded. If satisfaction is not achieved, then the grievance should be reported to head of year/head of department and then through to senior administrators, where the matter should be finally resolved.

Occasionally, a dissatisfied parent will attempt to short-circuit the protocol and speak to a trustee who, rather than direct the person to the head, seizes upon the cause for ulterior purposes.

The board member with a similar mindset as the parent, and, usually with an axe to grind against the head, decides to use this case as a *cause célèbre* to seek the removal of the head. Just as a healthy body can be destroyed by the entry of a single bacterium or virus, heads do sometimes lose their jobs because of the vindictiveness of a single board member.

In the majority of instances, the parent and/or board member will seek to gain support from other similarly-minded individuals, who will readily supply more negative fuel to the fire being kindled against the head. School car parks are ideal breeding grounds for such plots! Once a pressure group has been formed, a momentum develops and a campaign against the head is unleashed. Thereafter, the course and outcome of the campaign will depend upon the strength of the chair and head in combating the negativity arising from the dispute.

A pressure group of disaffected parents acts like a tumour within the organisation of the school. Alliances develop and in-groups and out-groups develop, each adding fuel to the list of woes to be thrown at the head. Once the board is infected, there is little hope that the matter will be speedily and successfully concluded without the satisfaction of blood being spilt, usually the head's.

Some boards have a membership drawn mainly from one organisation. In such situations, corporate status plays a large part in board dynamics. The views and desires of more senior colleagues can take precedence over those of more junior or recently elected colleagues. In some boards, the chair may assume such a level of autocracy through their position that no one dares challenge their views, including the head.

Sometimes the dissatisfaction with the head and their management performance/style stems from a parent, who may have decided to be nominated for the board simply with the express desire to get rid of the head. Here again, the principle of attracting a support base from other potentially disaffected governors is applied and once the base is strong enough the board is challenged with pressure to remove the head.

How can this be prevented?

Dealing with conflict is a tiresome and wearying process which can largely be avoided if the precipitating issue is handled dispassionately at an early stage by the head and chair.

An experienced head knows the dangers of disaffected parents and staff and knows they are an ever present threat. They will always stay vigilant, knowing that there are wolves prowling around their territory. Heads must be on the lookout for dissatisfaction within the parent body and within the staff. Rather than hope that problems will go away with time, they would be well advised to grasp the nettle and meet the problem head on with tact, diplomacy and tenacity at the first hint of trouble; certainly before a pressure group has a chance to form. It is easier to hit one target than several.

It is good practice to invite the disgruntled parent in for a meeting and allow the person to 'blow off steam', to 'get it off their chest'. Never meet more than one parent or pair of parents at the same time.

Encourage the person to express their feelings freely and encourage the feelings to come out as much as the substantive details of the issue. This is an important cathartic moment for the person. As feelings, emotions and bitterness pour out the head is going a long way towards resolving the issue. Better let the person have a field day at this stage than later. Exercise patience. Hear the person out. Do not interrupt and do not be defensive. Express concern and offer an element of sympathy. Ask for time to investigate the issues raised with colleagues and fix a date to meet the person again within a short period of time. This gives the head time to investigate the matter with all concerned, be apprised of the situation and provide time to develop a strategy to handle the disaffected parent/member of staff. It is also a good plan to inform the chair of actions taken, preferably in the form of a memo as opposed to verbally.

Meet the person again and report back on your findings. Reassure the person of your desire to find a just and equitable solution to the issue. Try to find something positive to say which is based on the original concern and know in advance how far, as head, you are prepared to go. Always seek reconciliation, as time and effort taken at this point will avoid hours of heartache later and often turn a sceptical parent into an ardent supporter.

If a problem is brought straight to the attention of the chair by a parent or staff member, they should refer the person to the appropriate member of staff/management for resolution and inform that person and the head of the approach.

In the event of criticism from a vociferous, disgruntled parent, a strong chair will invite the person to meet with them in the presence of the head and hear out the matter in the manner prescribed above. At all times the chair must support the head and make this clear to the disaffected person. A chair can only criticise the actions of a head when evidence against the head has been presented and verified, then this must be done in terms of the disciplinary procedure of the head's employment agreement.

Good communication, the free flow of information, confidentiality and discretion between board, chair and head, are essential in minimising situations likely to give rise to conflict. Heads, in particular, should never take anything for granted in their dealings with the board. Rather, they should ensure the board members fully understand the nature and implications of corporate decisions and actions, and ensure that these are reported and recorded accurately in all board minutes.

For effective governance to take place, the relationship between governance and administration must be clearly articulated. The roles, responsibilities and expectations of trustees and managers must form the basis of a written contract held by all parties. The chair, the head and each board member should be required to sign a memo of agreement which outlines and delimits their roles, their relationships and a protocol to follow in the event of disputes arising. Annual training in good governance too, is essential to maintaining effective working relationships.

Further, it should be recognised that the governance/administration relationship exists within a framework of mutual trust and respect, if not for individuals, then for roles. The transient nature of board membership, implications arising from changes in headship and the potential implications for conflict arising from such transitions should be recognised. Safeguards should be built into the governance/management dynamic to ensure smooth operation of the school in the event of these events.

Conflict resolution in governance and administration

Many incidents have been reported recently where a school has had a very successful head for a number of years and because of a change in chair or in board membership, the head has come under serious attack from the board. Often the situation was predicated by one or two trivial events. Without a policy on conflict resolution being in place in the school, the situation deteriorated, a state of destructive conflict (Deutsch, 1973) arose and the head was fired.

Upon reflection, all parties agreed that this was a complete lose/lose situation which caused the schools and individuals much harm. If a carefully thought out policy for conflict resolution had been in place in the school, supported by one of the professional international education membership organisations under whose patronage the school existed, damage could have been prevented or at least minimised.

Conflict resolution is a rapidly developing branch of the social sciences. Its origins are in antiquity, but events following the Second World War, notably the Cold War and Middle East tensions, and events within large multinational organisations have proved the benefit of conflict resolution expertise and intervention.

It is recommended that board policy and heads' contracts make provision for the implementation of conflict resolution intervention.

Schellenberg (1996) defines conflict resolution as '... a marked reduction in social conflict as a result of a conscious settlement of issues in dispute.' In order to achieve resolution to a conflict there has to be a conscious decision on the part of all concerned to effect a settlement. Once a situation in school has developed to the extent that the initial attempts that have been made within the board framework to resolve issues have failed, a dispute should be declared either by the head or the chair, and a process of mediation begun.

Mediation can only take place in an atmosphere in which conflicting parties voluntarily seek for resolution and where there is common agreement on protection of joint interests, fairness and closure.

Mediation is the least threatening form of contraposition resolution by virtue of its simplicity and the clarity of its rules. It is essentially an informal method of dispute resolution in which a neutral third party, the mediator, attempts, using the technique of cooperative constructive conflict resolution, to assist two or more parties to achieve an agreement, with concrete effects, on a matter of common interests to the parties.

The mediator has no coercive role in the process. Any resolution reached between the two parties is under the control of the parties and stems from their desire to conclude the conflict with minimum damage to both parties.

There is a growing belief that such a service should be provided by professional international education membership organisations. In the case of schools which are accredited by such an organisation, a board policy requiring the school to implement conflict resolution intervention as and when required ought to be a *sine qua non* for accreditation. Such a situation would avoid so much unnecessary damage to member schools.

Bibliography

Coser, L (1956) *The Functions of Social Conflict*. NY: Free Press.

Council for International schools (2004) Board Governance Newsletter Volume 2 No.2. NY: CIS.

Deutsch, M (1973) *The Resolution of Conflict*. New Haven: Yale University Press.

Hawley, D (1994) How long do International school heads survive? Part 1. *International schools Journal* XIV (1), pp.8-21.

Hawley, D (1995) How long do International school heads survive? Part 2. *International schools Journal* XIV, (2), pp.23-36.

Littleford, J & Associates (1999) *The Governance Game*. Littleford and Associates.

Schellenberg, J A (1996) *Conflict Resolution Theory, Research and Practice*. NY.

Schoppert, G (2002) Governing Boards: how do they function? *International School*, 4 (2), pp.11-12.

Chapter Eight

The board and evaluation

'He who knows others is wise; he who knows himself is enlightened.' Lao-tz (541–479 BC)

In this chapter the emphasis will lie in providing a framework for the regular evaluation of board performance and progress.

Throughout the book we have referred to the board's key responsibilities. Many board members understand these intellectually but frequently their actions are contradictory. CIS has laid down certain performance expectations, and it is intended that governance will play an increasingly important role in the accreditation process. Let us therefore briefly recap on the role of the board:

- To determine policy and strategy.
- To exercise trusteeship in terms of financial responsibility.
- To appoint and evaluate the head.

The role of the board chair is:

- To lead the board of trustees to make wise decisions with regard to the three activities shown above.
- To plan meetings, manage trustees, keep the focus on what is important and strategic.
- To approve the appointment of the head of school and to support and liaise with the head thereafter.

Research conducted by Dr Ross H Millikan shows that high quality student outcomes come from continuity, stability, competence and confidence in the leadership provided by the board chair and head in particular. Millikan also writes about the tendency within International schools of board members demonstrating a desire 'to leave their mark on the organization'. He suggests that short term tenure in key board positions can sometimes result in undue haste in pursuing issues or goals. Experience tends to make many of us believe that short-term board tenure often results in paralysis or heightens the desire to achieve rapid change.

This is why it is so important that a strategic board constantly reflects on whether their strategic plan and their actions are in line with the vision, mission and values of the school. This reflection can only be articulated into positive data if there are regular evaluations of progress and behavior.

Evaluation procedures, no matter what their format, should cover the range and balance of activities in which the board is involved. A strong element of the evaluation should reflect the board's relationship with the head of school and their knowledge of the context in which the school operates.

While no evaluation system applies equally well to all schools the samples included in this book can be adjusted and modified. Many schools have an excellent annual evaluation procedure but do not discuss or deal with the results. Boards sometimes hide behind the excuse that the data refers to last year's board and chair and is therefore not pertinent to the new board. Whatever the results, they impact on the quality of the school and as such must be recognised and addressed.

The trustees' committee should be the guardian of the evaluation process and the findings. All circulated evaluation forms and questionnaires should be signed. Anonymous expressions of opinion are not acceptable. The board should:

- Evaluate itself.
- Invite the head and the administration to evaluate the board.
- Evaluate the board chair.
- Incorporate the findings into the governance section of the annual review of the strategic plan.

Regardless of the approach you use to evaluate, it must be measured against a clear and detailed statement of expectations. Try to always keep in mind that a busy board is not always an effective board. Be strategic and make your time count.

Evaluation process

It is essential to look at each of the evaluations in context with one another because each one is part of a whole and each one impacts on the other.

Ideally the board should with the help of a facilitator discuss the strengths and weaknesses identified in the review and incorporate it into the annual board training. This method helps the group to establish the criteria and indicators for improvement. One vital part of the process is to evaluate the performance of all members coming up for re-election or re-appointment, to confirm their continuing suitability. This necessarily implies that the trustees' committee has the duty to recommend to the board that underperforming members should stand down.

All the forms given here have been used in different International schools. We would advise you to adapt them to meet your own particular situation and needs. It is important that the evaluation forms you use produce meaningful information and do not irritate or alienate. Once you have devised forms that work there are huge advantages to using the same approach each year, with any necessary modifications to reflect changed circumstances.

We offer up for your consideration:

- a board evaluation form;
- a board chair evaluation form;
- a head of school evaluation form;
- potential board candidate criteria for choice.

We have deliberately included a board candidate criteria form to encourage boards to think more strategically when inviting people to stand as candidates or considering them for appointment. This useful tool will enable the nominating committee to be sure that as far as is humanly possible the members have chosen the right person for the right reasons.

Important pitfalls to avoid in evaluation

1. You are evaluating the quality of performance and not being judgmental of people.
2. Measure against clear and agreed goals and not your own perceptions.
3. The evaluation should be based on what is best for the school – not you.
4. Do not seek to impose your views rather than the findings of the evaluation on others.

Board chair evaluation

We are frequently asked what the key responsibility of the board chair is. Our answer to this question is straightforward. The role of the board chair is to lead and direct the board so as to ensure the long-term viability and future of the school. To achieve this goal the board chair must:

- Be passionate about the school's vision and mission and inspire others.
- Be committed and have the ability to attract commitment.
- Listen and hear.

The four major skills required are:

- The ability to facilitate and develop a group process.
- The ability to develop and manage relationships.
- The ability to plan and evaluate.
- The ability to communicate.

When evaluating the board chair it is important to follow these guidelines:

- The evaluation to be successful must be undertaken within the context of the history, character, and culture of the school.
- The evaluation must be used to allow the school to build on the board chair's strengths and to provide a supportive process to lessen the impact of the weaknesses.

Head of school evaluation

It is still surprising in this complex modern world that heads of school are sadly either not evaluated or the evaluation is superficial and without real value. The head of school should not only be evaluated by the board but also by the members of the senior administration team. The latter would receive a questionnaire to complete and return. This would be evaluated and form part of the board committee's evaluation. We suggest the following procedure could be of use to your school. The board chair circulates a short questionnaire to the board members and then sets up a small committee to conduct the evaluation interview process. This committee would normally consist of the board chair, treasurer, chair of the trustees committee and one other.

The timing of this meeting is usually late spring and the core of the discussion should break down into three areas:

- the head of school's goals and indicators of success;
- the head's self evaluation;
- the feedback from the senior administrators' questionnaires.

The meeting should be constructive and well-balanced, identifying and praising areas of success and seeking to find solutions to under-performance. Both areas of weaknesses and strengths should be incorporated in the head's schoolwide and personal goals for the coming year.

The board should receive from the head of school feedback on the process in a written and oral format.

The final duty of the committee is to decide the level of the head's compensation for the coming year. If the head's contract has only one more year to run then formal contract renewal or non renewal should be part of that duty.

Conclusion

The evaluation process should not appear to be daunting or bureaucratic but more an essential activity that helps you to know more about yourself, the school and, if you are a trustee, the board within which you operate. Knowledge and information are some of the tools an effective board needs to develop, so that they can be of service and productive. The goal must always be to re-enforce the culture of a Community of Learners!

Chapter Nine

Final review

Every International school board of trustees wants to do well, but the reality is that few have the time, knowledge or opportunity to fulfil their potential. Many inherit built in problems and complex structures, and lack the visionary leadership to guide them to strategic thinking. Most of us do not appreciate how the introduction of one new board member can shift the board's attitude and approach to its duties, especially if the member is motivated by self-interest and the board has weak leadership. Too many boards fail to take impartial help or training. If this sounds overly judgmental then please forgive us.

To truly succeed you must not only build a strong and united team that is ready to focus on the strategic issues, but also an ongoing support infrastructure to support this mindset. Dr Meredith Belbin defines a team role as 'a tendency to behave, contribute and interrelate with others in a particular way'. This affects how each board member interrelates with the others and this in turn affects the progress of the team. We would therefore like to suggest that it is of benefit to board members to look at their core individual personality traits, intellectual and cultural styles, and behaviour patterns, and reflect on the implications this has for the team. Belbin's research shows that there are nine team roles and their presence or lack of presence does much to define a team's success. These team roles break down into three groupings:

- the action orientated roles;
- the people oriented roles;
- the cerebral roles.

Boards that become distracted by trivia or operational issues, and fail to evaluate their annual performance, are not working within the philosophy of good governance for International schools. Trustees are accountable and must constantly review the implications of their actions, and allow others to judge their performance.

Boards are not there to dictate the answers: their role is to question, monitor and focus on the vision, mission and values of the school. Mark Light in his book the *Strategic Board*, quotes Sharon Percy Rockefeller, CEO of WETA in Washington. The most important thing Sharon Percy Rockefeller learned upon joining the board of the University of Stanford was that a good board member continuously asks 'why?'

We would also like to stress the importance of improving the selection process of board members. Avoid thinking 'we'll be lucky if we get anyone – so let's take who we can'! Really research, cultivate and groom potential board members so that they are ready to take on their role. Try to avoid only training people after they are elected.

We sincerely hope that regardless of the form of governance operating in your school you have found the book to be of interest and help. Being a board member, and holding the school in trust, is an enormous responsibility and one not to be undertaken lightly. It demands the same level of dedication associated with top team sports people. This dedication requires continuous training, an understanding of your own strengths and weaknesses and those of your fellow members, performance evaluation and mental and physical harmony.

We also hope that the concept of the integrated team – the board plus the head and senior administrators working together – will be the future way forward.

We wish you all well.

Bibliography

Belbin, Dr Meridith (1993) *Team Roles at Work*. Butterworth Heinemann.
Light, Mark *The Strategic Board*. Wiley Not for Profit Series.

Appendix

Contents

1. Board Candidate Criteria for choice.................................... 51
2. Board of trustees evaluation questionnaire.......................... 52
3. Board chair evaluation 53
4. Head of school evaluation 55

Appendix 1

Board candidate criteria for choice

Please ensure that the candidate you recommend satisfactorily meets at least 75% of these points.

1. Has this person consistently demonstrated an active interest or involvement in the school? How would you measure this interest?

2. How well do you know this person or the person who nominated him/her?

   very well   an acquaintance   not at all

3. What in your opinion are the main attributes that this person will bring to the board?

4. What would you describe as this person's greatest strength?

5. Has this person previous experience as a trustee?

6. What team characteristics do you believe this person possesses?

7. How would you describe this person's style of communication?

8. Would this person be prepared to donate to a school fundraising initiative?

9. What spheres of influence and support could this person bring to the school?

10. Will this person's style complement those of the other board members?

11. Is this person a potential board officer? If so, state which.

Appendix 2

Board of trustees evaluation questionnaire

To be completed by trustees only.

Please rate the board's performance in relation to these statements: 5 (high) 1 (low)

1. We organise the work of the board to enable us to act strategically and not operationally.
2. We regularly review progress against agreed indicators.
3. Our committees discuss issues and options connected to their role.
4. We leave detailed discussions to committee meetings.
5. We understand the difference between the head of school's role and that of a trustee.
6. We have a planned programme for policy review.
7. We participate in regular governance training.
8. Our board orientation programme meets the needs of new members.
9. Board meetings are timely and effective.
10. We always consider alternative scenarios when making decisions.
11. The minutes of the open session of the board meetings are circulated to the internal stakeholders.
12. We participate in an annual evaluation process and publish the results.
13. We use the evaluation results to improve our performance.
14. We set annual goals for the board and its committees.
15. We regularly update our strategic plan.
16. We seek to prevent personal bias affecting our decisions.

Further comments:

Appendix 3

Board chair evaluation questionnaire

This evaluation form can be used in a number of different ways. It can be distributed to board members in advance of the meeting when the chair's evaluation will be on the agenda so that individuals can complete it independently. The results can then be tabulated and discussed. Alternatively, it can serve as a discussion guide for the board as it engages in a group appraisal of the board chair's performance.

Directions

The following statements describe a variety of leadership and management practices which the chair may employ in the course of carrying out his/her responsibilities. Please consider to what extent the statement is true and circle the appropriate ranking below.

> 1:Never 2:Rarely 3:Only Occasionally 4:Sometimes: 5:Frequently 6:Almost Always 7:Always

1	Given the attached description of the chair's role, how well does the present board chair fulfil that role?	1 2 3 4 5 6 7
2	Is the board chair approachable?	1 2 3 4 5 6 7
3	Is the board chair flexible and open to new ideas?	1 2 3 4 5 6 7
4	How well does the board chair meet stated expectations in his/her relationship with a. the head? b. the board of trustees? c. the school's stakeholders?	1 2 3 4 5 6 7 1 2 3 4 5 6 7 1 2 3 4 5 6 7
5	Does the board chair manage meetings effectively and allow others to contribute fully?	1 2 3 4 5 6 7
6	Is the board chair's leadership style consistent with the described role?	1 2 3 4 5 6 7
7	Does the board chair meet stated performance outcomes and encourage board training?	1 2 3 4 5 6 7

8	Does the board chair meet expected professional standards?	1 2 3 4 5 6 7
9	Is the relationship between the board chair and the head such that each can communicate openly and frankly?	1 2 3 4 5 6 7
10	Does the board chair inspire confidence and trust?	1 2 3 4 5 6 7
11	Is the board chair articulate and able to communicate with all the school's stakeholders?	1 2 3 4 5 6 7
12	As a board member do you feel a genuine sense of progress and achievement?	1 2 3 4 5 6 7

Further Comments:

Appendix 4

Head of school evaluation questionnaire

To be completed by board members and senior administrators.

Please grade 7 (high) to 1 (low).

1. Do the head's activities live up to and reflect the school's mission, values and vision?
2. Does the head ensure that the board is kept up to date and well informed about his/her activities?
3. Does the head provide the board with the necessary school information to ensure their effectiveness?
4. Does the head show forward-looking leadership in ensuring the school's future?
5. Does the head show sufficient financial acumen to effectively manage the school's financial affairs?
6. Does the head work well with the board chair and the chairs of the board committees?
7. Does the head work well with the senior administration team and ensure that their activities are both beneficial and appropriate to the school's mission, values and vision?
8. Does the head work well with other stakeholder groups, both internally and externally?
9. Does the head ensure that the school's professional development program promotes the school's mission, values and vision?
10. Did the head achieve the goals set for the school year?
11. Did the head effectively represent the school in the external environment?
12. Does the head have a clear overview of what is happening in the school?
13. Is the head accessible?
14. Is the head able to delegate effectively?

Further Comments:

Notes

Notes

Notes

Notes

Notes

Notes

Notes

Notes